THE LAST DREAM-O-RAMA

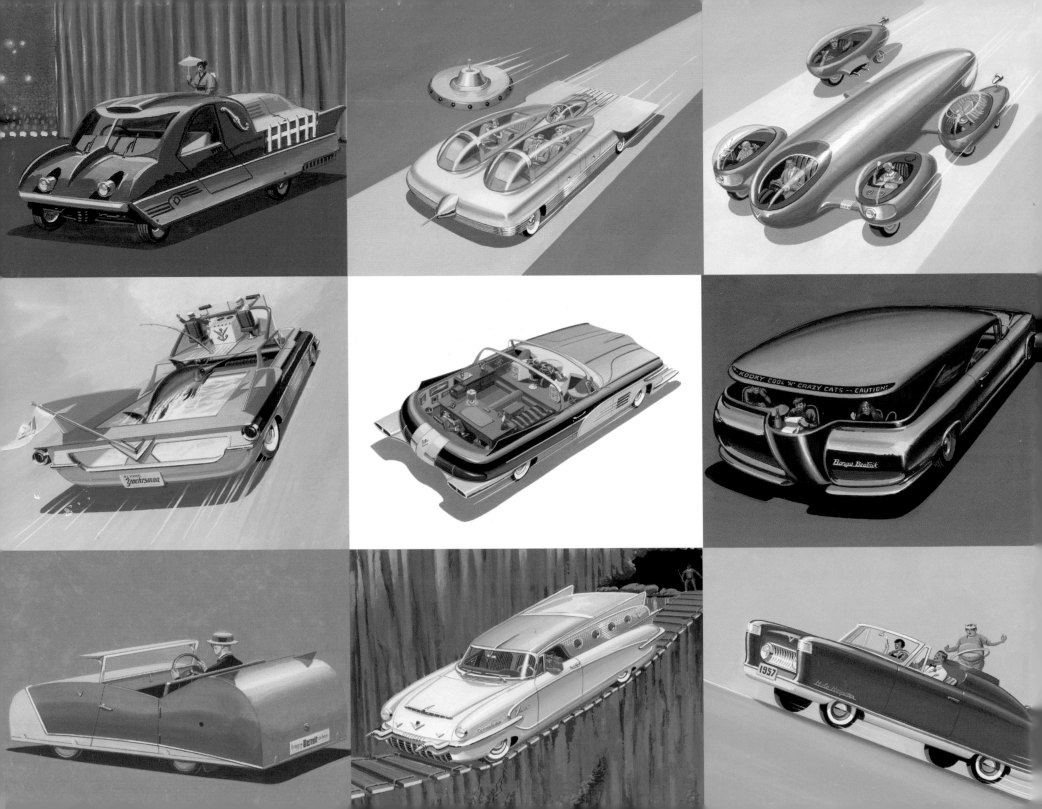

THE LAST DREAM-O-RAMA

THE CARS DETROIT FORGOT TO BUILD, 1950-1960

By Bruce McCall

Crown Publishers
New York

Published by Crown Publishers, New York, New York. Member of the Crown Publishing Group.

Random House, Inc. New York, Toronto, London, Sydney, Auckland
www.randomhouse.com

CROWN is a trademark and the Crown colophon is a registered trademark of Random House, Inc.

Printed in China

Design by Kay Schuckhart/Blond on Pond

Library of Congress Cataloging-in-Publication Data
McCall, Bruce.
The last dream-o-rama: the cars Detroit forgot to build, 1950–1960/by Bruce McCall.—1st ed.
   1. Automobiles—Humor.   2. Automobiles—Caricatures and cartoons.   3. American wit and humor, pictorial. I. Title.
PN6231.A8 M37 2001
818'.5402—dc21   00-046590

ISBN 0-609-60801-0

10 9 8 7 6 5 4 3 2 1

First Edition

CONTENTS

INTRODUCTION

This book really began more than forty years ago in my cubicle at the commercial art studio where I spent most of the Fifties. I was a prodigy of incompetence at the craft of painting luscious pictures of new cars for magazines and catalogs, which meant infrequent assignments, which opened up plentiful time for reflection. From my front-row seat I reflected often on Detroit's trivialization of that complex thing called the automobile into a form of popular entertainment and instant kitsch. You can read a culture in its cars, and judging by the cars of that time, American culture was in a state. The yardstick of excellence lost out to the thrill of novelty. Ads competed for most frequent use of the word *new,* as in "New!!!," even while the technology within that insanely ornate outer shell grew mossy from neglect. If the American car world of that era were a planet, it would be covered with a layer of deep superficiality and have a vacuum at its core. Detroit bloated up on profits from the worst-built, worst-designed, worst-handling, all-round worst cars in the civilized world. And for all anybody knew back in the Fifties, it would go on this way forever. Or as long as the supplies of chrome and vinyl and four-inch whitewall tires held up.

I hope the cars, ideas, and values that permeate the pages of this book can even approach the originals that inspired them in their fatuousness, bad taste, and shameless excess.

Detroit and its antics in the Fifties—so almost innocently witless, so endearingly crass—inspire something close to affection today. Not so the Fifties themselves. Not my Fifties. The haze of fond nostalgia that now enshrouds this middle decade of the twentieth century suggests that for many Americans it was a halcyon period. Well, there were probably people who thrived during the Black Plague, too. Even from my peephole perspective, sealed in that studio in a gritty Canadian border city year after year, the Fifties were obviously and unrelentingly bleak. I still see that decade as fabulous only in how long it stayed in its stupor of mediocrity. So much as the sound of doo-wop, the mention of Arthur Godfrey or Tab Hunter or Senator Joseph McCarthy or John Foster Dulles, the mere idea of a white sport coat and a pink carnation can set me off all over again today. If the Fifties sensibility and style recreated herein strike the reader as even half as dismally moronic as they were at the time, doing this book won't have been in vain.

I wish to acknowledge the primary role played by others in bringing this book to life. It began with an idea donated by my agent, Liz Darhansoff, which I worked up into an elaborate proposal promptly passed upon by some of the brightest minds in book publishing before it wandered into Crown. There, Steve Ross glimpsed a better idea hiding behind the original, and after overcoming my bruised pride, so did I. Doug Pepper, also of Crown, figured out how to make it all happen, and my wife, Polly, waited patiently while I hibernated in my office for some months, slaving to improve upon the same skills with brush and paint that had been found so wanting four decades ago. The results may not shimmer as artwork, but they certainly taste sweet as revenge.

THE AMERICAN DREAM DRIVES

OFF IN ALL DIRECTIONS

Car-minded? Americans had had cars on their brains, not to mention gasoline in their blood and carbon monoxide in their lungs, for decades. And when the postwar economic boom fostered such prosperity that easy credit allowed even poor folks to plunge hopelessly into debt, a brand-new car at last became an attainable dream for millions.

Then something happened to supercharge those dreams and stimulate the automotive saliva glands till they foamed. The dream car arrived. Each one, one of a kind. Not for sale, hands off, here today only to be gone tomorrow. But the dream car would quickly become as beloved a part of Fifties life as President Eisenhower's heart attacks and rigged TV game shows. By mid-decade every American carmaker was parading its glittering glimpses of four-wheeled futurism before a dazzled public—flights of styling fancy and functional wonderment blaring "Headed for your driveway soon!" while mumbling "Don't hold us to it." The industry had never had it so good: By 1954 there

OPPOSITE: Opening night of Matterhorn Motors' Futurific Tomorrowrama Cavalcade of Chrome, Detroit, October 1954. Public hysteria topped Orson Welles's 1938 radio broadcast of *War of the Worlds* before Matterhorn announced that none of the dream cars on display would be produced for sale.

BELOW: A typical no-frills auto show in the pre-dream-car era. Organizers paid visitors to attend but lacked funds to advertise time and place, so few did. Note money-saving natural light.

were five tires for every car in America and a new car sold for every one built. Contrast this with the 1946 Detroit Auto Show, staged in an unused corner of the downtown Christian Science Reading Room without disturbing a Christian, a Scientist, or a Reader. Yet a mere eight years later, an itch in time, Matterhorn Motors' touring Futurific Tomorrowrama Cavalcade of Chrome was packing rented hotel ballrooms from Bangor to Rognab

with glamour and glitz so newer-than-new that tomorrow suddenly seemed like yesterday.

Detroit's dream cars mirrored the aspirations of

mid-century America with uncanny, almost bone-chilling accuracy. And scant wonder. In a nation that now had the H-bomb, Cinerama, and chloro-

OPPOSITE: The 1955 Cavalcade of Chrome turns New York's Penn Station into a wonderland of canned music, lost tots, and five-dollar Cokes.

BELOW: Inside Bulgemobile's top-security dream-car styling studio, circa 1955. Executives scrutinize a full-size clay mock-up, while out of camera range, nervous stylists vomit. A thumbs-down on their handiwork and the giant overhead Cruncholator would flatten the model into a plasticine pizza, ready for sculpting into another try.

Every dream car was a team effort among the magicians of the Advanced Styling section—as exemplified in this half-finished preliminary sketch. Myriad individual concepts good-naturedly battle for dominance as, in alphabetical order, each team member steps up to try his hand.

phyll chewing gum, it didn't take a seer to know that Americans were dreaming big and bold and brassy. And wanted cars to match. Meanwhile, the miracle of motivational research could now ferret out people's innermost fears and lusts, to be manipulated by messages hidden in chrome and steel. The automobile was no longer just an appliance but a rolling boudoir, a metal mistress, a leather-clad dominatrix with great big pointed silver bumpers. And the industry's leaders had the vision to follow the mob. "Conformity, materialism, status, sex, insularity,

greed—what a country!" So exulted the chairman of Matterhorn Motors at a Senate hearing on a bill to ban foreign cars. And so did every dream car by Matterhorn and every maker dramatize a theme as now, as newsy as the latest CIA-run overthrow of the government of a distant land. Pontefract's 1956 Flash-Flair 2000QX Quadrabolt, for example, dramatizing the hot new concept of planned obsolescence, was designed to fall apart within six months and so accelerate its owner's need to car-shop again. Bulgemobile's Dixiecrat Twinstar of the following

year celebrated the popular concept of "separate but equal" race relations with a white car up front and a black car behind, exactly equal in trunk space.

Yet not everything about American life in the Fifties made a theme ideal for tickling the buying impulse. There were, it transpired, such things as too commercial a spin, too sharp a point. Showgoers' responses to certain dream cars accordingly wavered—and even, as in the case of Chundle's dramatic but dramatically flawed 1957 KKK Fire-Cross, backfired.

Such dreams gone awry were quickly gone from view and never publicly mentioned again. But lost to posterity forever? Thankfully not. A jimmied door, a rifled file case, a bulging folder innocently labeled "Old Lady Buying Habits, 1955–57"—paydirt! In the following pages, Detroit's buried mistakes—the rancid cream of those dream cars–turned–nightmares from forty-odd years ago—are exhumed for one last look and a brief wallow in forensic nostalgia.

Through these forgotten cars and the issues, enthusiasms, and yes, berserk obsessions that inspired them, perhaps we can recover something of the tenor of those fabulous Fifties. History on wheels, it might be termed. Fatuous, phony, tasteless history it may be; but hey, we're not talking some Golden Age here. We're talking the Fifties.

Epilogue in slime: By 1962, the dream-car era was over and discarded marvels rot in a watery open grave behind Bulgemobile's suburban Detroit styling complex, which today is the site of Swampleigh Court Estates, a gated community. Hauntingly, residents often report finding chrome bezels and V-shaped ornaments in their bathroom bowls.

DREAM CARS OF THE FIFTIES:

THE GOLDEN AGE OF INSOMNIA

Kamoda K-1 Sightseer, Circa 1941

Was this flyweight little open roadster history's first dream car? Historians differ. The K-1 was certainly one of a kind, it was not for sale, and with its spring-powered, key-wound motor, the all-tin Japanese import epitomized dream-car innovation. But it appeared at no auto shows, almost furtively avoided publicity, and vanished overnight only weeks after first being spotted. The few known facts are these: In Hawaii in November of 1941 a Japanese freighter unloads, and a representative from the Japanese Consulate claims, what is listed on the ship's manifest as "one Sightseeing Motorcar with Nose-Mounted Tourist Camera," built at Yokohama's giant Kamoda Saucer and Button Works. The cute little flivver and its lone driver are frequently spotted parked in the Pearl Harbor area. He explains to friendly passersby that the K-1's spring-powered motor can only move it two or three hundred yards per wind-up and that those wind-ups are hard work, requiring rest periods to recover. But he hopes to complete his sightseeing by early December. Honolulans by the score happily pose for that ingenious nose-mounted camera, complete with telescopic lens—and always against a colorful backdrop of U.S. Navy ships and docks. Then comes the Day of Infamy, December 7, 1941. The K-1 is destroyed in the Japanese sneak attack—it must have been, because neither it nor its driver is ever seen again.

Atomikar, 1947

The promise of atomic power for peaceful uses hovered on the American horizon like a mushroom cloud of hope in 1947 when Monolith Motors unveiled the world's first atomic-powered car and Detroit's first-ever dream car. And a working prototype, at that. True, the Atomikar's bulky core reactor did bump up curb weight to tons in the double figures, while melting the asbestos floor mats and the driver's shoes. A 12-mile-per-hour top speed and estimated running cost of $3 million per mile did flout established norms, but M.M. engineers believed such glitches could be licked over time. That time so abruptly ran out cannot be entirely blamed on crude technology. How could the engineers—how could anyone at the time—know what those running sores and that peeling skin shared by everyone who had ever come within fifty feet of the Atomikar really betokened? Dream car–turned–nightmare, some aver. But a simple sign out in the desert near Los Alamos, New Mexico, commemorates the Atomikar's bold pioneering for all time. BEWARE!, it reads. RADIATION DANGER FROM BURIED OBJECT! KEEP AWAY!

Glamoramic Polo Lounger Funtop, 1954

Hollywood agents since the days of the silents had been accused of giving sleaze a bad name, and they were finally fed up. Time for image work: ads, PR releases, charitable donations—even a dream car. That money might have passed under the table between the agents and Pontefract Corp. could never be proven. Beyond question is that the Funtop backfired in its mission to alter the rep of moviedom's hustling ten-percenters. Something about the basic styling theme? Certainly that removable Funtop, duplicating a Brylcreemed hairpiece, and tinted aviator shades in lieu of the conventional windshield sent mixed messages at best. The blinding white smile on that porcelain grille struck many as a tad insincere. And Hollywood agent credibility probably was not enhanced by a speedometer that exaggerated the Polo Lounger's speed by 50 miles per hour. Had Bulgemobile captured the spirit of agentry all too well? Philosophers may differ; for their part, the agents evidently believed as much. They sued Pontefract for defamation of character, losing their case only at the Supreme Court level, when the nine justices ruled that agents had no character to defame.

Buckingham RR Westminster Silver Spoon Brougham, 1953

Rolls-Royce the world's most coveted automobile? Not if Matterhorn Motors had anything to say about it! Carved from a single iron ingot, the openly derivative Silver Spoon vied to wrest that distinction from the historic English marque's grasp with brash American confidence—studded with such unmistakably Olde English accents as a pedigreed bulldog resident in the boot and a roll-out Axminster parking carpet. Matterhorn's obsession with Rolls-Royce and world-class status was not, alas, the show-going American public's. Visitors to the Westminster stand keenly resented the posted order to bow or curtsy, while Matterhorn's ridicule of Queen Elizabeth II for being "too yellow" to drag-race her Daimler limousine against the U.S. challenger drew scathing editorials—even in Pravda. Especially after Her Majesty finally accepted the dare and won.

Redscare Phantom Witchhunter, 1954

Bulgemobile Corp.'s fear of the U.S. Senate Subcommittee on Anti-Patriotic Influences allegedly stemmed from the fact that the company had built and sold more red cars since the onset of the Cold War than any other American manufacturer. In the climate of the times, a public accusation of harboring pro-Soviet sympathies would be a business catastrophe. Out of this PR pickle came one of the more unusual dream cars of the Fifties. The Phantom Witchhunter, presented as a gift to the subcommittee, was "a rolling hearing room," brayed Bulgemobile press handouts, "supplemented by surveillance mikes and cameras and even fitted with a drop-slot for anonymous tips, so patriotic citizens can expose loved ones, friends, and neighbors as Soviet stooges when the Redscare passes through their hometowns." What some left-wing editorialists smeared as shameless truckling worked. Bulgemobile ducked the Commie-lover stigma—though its red-paint option has been named "Bunker Hill Scarlet" ever since.

Silver Sabre Patriomatic Funfighter, 1951

If the Korean Conflict is all but forgotten today, where does that leave the Silver Sabre? Commemorating a stalemated U.N. police action on the Korean Peninsula with a civilian American dream car was possibly a case of patriotic fervor winning out over commercial appeal. The single-seat Silver Sabre, with its jet-fighter styling, aircraft-type cockpit, simulated aerodynamics, and a gunsight-type hood ornament that flipped up to reveal a cigarette lighter, did make a dramatic sight. But its day in the sun proved to be cloudy, with early showers. After negative response at auto shows—perhaps influenced by the clever but misguided stagecraft that had it rolling over a battalion of stuntmen dressed as Chinese soldiers every hour on the hour—the Sabre was loaned to the U.S. Air Force as a recruiting tool, then went into mothballs when nine out of ten would-be recruits declined their free drives and joined the navy. Its final chapter proved to be its noblest: Purchased by the CIA at a tag sale, it was mailed to North Korea with no return address in 1959 as an experiment in psychological warfare.

Quizfire 5000 Jackpot, 1956

TV quiz shows and the lure of huge cash jackpots just for knowing the capital of Albania were a mid-Fifties national obsession, and the spectacular Quizfire 5000 was designed to take it on the road. It was a natural— one dream of material excess intermixed with another. The car itself was far from the only reward of driving, Quizfire-style. Its driver and sole occupant, snug inside his very own soundproof isolation booth, was linked by radiotelephone to the emcee of NBC's *Million-Dollar Moment* and could instantly win five thousand dollars in cash if the Quizfire happened to be in a preselected "Secret City" when a gong sounded during the show. When the sordid truth was spilled by a disgruntled ex-stylist—the Secret Cities were all in Asia Minor—the Quizfire 5000's credibility, like that of those TV quiz shows, evaporated overnight.

El Scandinavia Mk XXX, 1956

"The Look of Today, Tomorrow!" was Matterhorn Motors' promotional theme for 1956, and semanticists, at least those with both the time and the inclination, still bicker over its precise meaning: a promise, or an IOU? Likewise, even granted the mid-Fifties Danish Modern furniture mania, the El Scandinavia's incorporation of so much blond wood in then-modish curvilinear forms—extending even to the oval-shaped coffee table shared by the driver and front passenger—long baffled the automotive design community. Frequent polishing was needed to maintain the wood's silky finish, and those extended wood shapes sweeping around the car's nose could be easily splintered in parking. Worse, what would happen when the Danish Modern craze—as must all crazes—waned? In the face of such glaring and obvious problems, why build the El Scandinavia at all? It was only in 1984 that Matterhorn's head of styling, long since retired and his confidentiality clause lapsed, at last "came clean." Nobody cared about splinters or waxing or the end of the trend, he revealed. Matterhorn had just moved into its new $435 million headquarters building back in '56, he explained, "and we had to do something with all that old office furniture, fast."

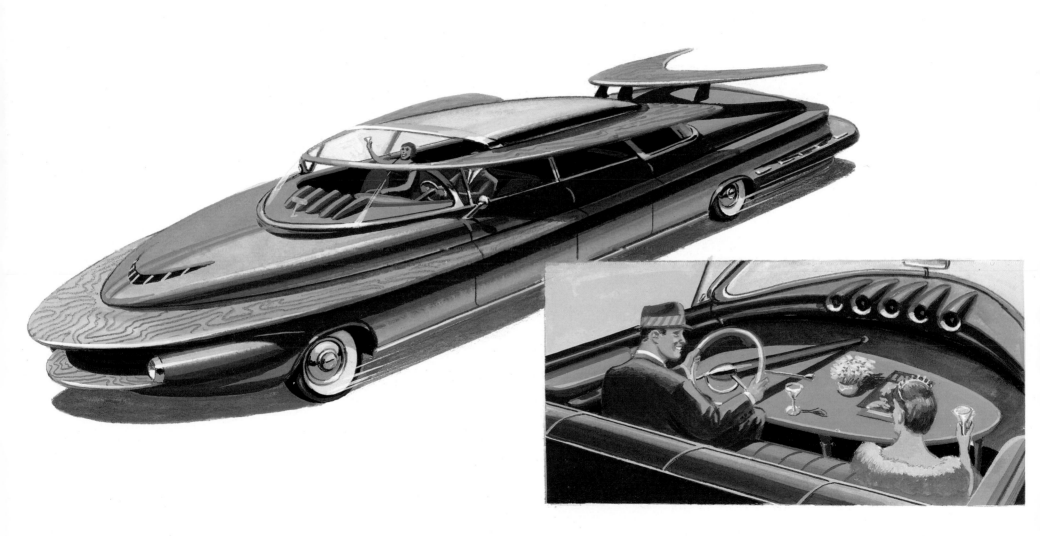

Panavista FilmFlyte Visionaire, 1955

Nine-abreast seating, popcorn machine in the glove box, a panoramic view of the world through the rose-tinted glass of its wraparound windshield: The Panavista aspired to nothing less than making a trip to the corner store the equal of the 3-D wide-screen movies Hollywood had just introduced to win back its waning audience from TV. This dreamiest of dream cars debuted at the world premiere of Mogultone Studios' 1955 spectacle, *Make Mine Mozambique!*, in Santa Monica, California. So wide that its occupants could watch three drive-in movies at once, the Panavista nonetheless betrayed fundamental flaws that prevented its ever advancing to production status. There were very few nine-member families to fill up its seats, for example, and the mass disruption whenever someone in the middle had to use the bathroom was never really solved. Movies might well be better than ever, as Hollywood crowed, but cars based on movie theaters still had a ways to go.

Rocketerra El Famiglia Multicar X4, 1957

Anything seemed possible in those balmy days of fluoridated drinking water and 3-D movies—why not a dream car so far-out that, at the touch of a push button, the occupant of any one of its four "Pow-R-Pods" could detach himself to go roaming the highways, then dock again with the "Dad Ship" when it was time to chow down or catch Arthur Godfrey on the radio headset? That, in a nutshell, was the Rocketerra El Famiglia Multicar X4. But that wasn't all. Mom's Pow-R-Pod was a self-contained kitchen, Sis's had its own TV, and the rear portside "Lav-A-Pod" was there to serve all three road-going riders whenever anybody tugged on the emergency cord and the X-4 screeched to a halt. With luggage space for a three-month vacation and a pipe rack for Dad with automatic pipe pop-up, what could this techno-miracle possibly lack? A rocket engine, for starters. And though folks understood when the engineers explained that such a power-plant was still years away, the letdown was palpable—and permanent—when the futuristic Rocketerra was revealed to be a pedal car.

FLYING Yachtsman

X-Trovert X-Quisite Silver Spray, 1955

"Dual-Deck Drive Command" was the X-Quisite's major innovation, allowing the driver and a lucky sidekick to shuttle at will between a conventional position inside the car and the Flying Bridge up top, making this bold dream car the star of both auto and powerboat shows. A swordfish-sized fishing tank, complete with live swordfish, obviated the need to go anywhere near the water, and the marine theme was carried through to a wooden ship's wheel for steering and, in place of an accelerator pedal, a speaking tube for ordering changes in speed to the "engine room" on the far side of the firewall via voice-activated solenoids. Less compelling were the X-Quisite's ride and handling, all too authentically similar to that floating and wallowing sensation often felt on the high seas, and "Powerboat-Smooth" braking, a controversial new feature requiring the driver to slow down by reversing the engine and coming to a full stop only by casting a line around a parking meter and pulling really hard.

Vegastar StripStreak Headliner Deluxe, 1958

Tragedy was to mar the glamour-filled career of the show-stopping Vegastar, the only dream car directly inspired by the emergence of Las Vegas as the fabulous epicenter of American entertainment. With its Vegas-style illuminated sign, a slot-machine gearshift, and a speedometer that showed three cherries when the car hit 100 miles per hour, the Vegastar was a self-contained private casino for Mom, Pop, and the kids. But when casino operator Bugsy Tarantula demanded to buy it, Monolith Motors said no; and when most of the company's head stylist was found in the trunk the next morning, fun turned to fear. Tensions might have become unbearable had associates not reported that Mr. Tarantula went hiking in the desert one night shortly afterward, spread-eagled himself on an anthill to rest, and accidentally shot himself nine times in the back of the head while cleaning his pistol in his sleep.

Togethercar FourPlay, 1955

"Togetherness" was a theme that oozed through American life in the Fifties like a barrel of spilled molasses. The Togethercar FourPlay, Chundle Motors' expression of that theme in dream-car form, brought the American family together at a whole new level of interaction, intimacy, and good-natured competition: parent versus parent, child versus child, children against their parents, parents against their children. Eight hands grabbing for control of one steering wheel taught the kids that grown-ups were stronger, and the grown-ups that kids didn't have driver's licenses for good reason. If four people careening down the road like bickering half-wits aboard a runaway circus wagon wasn't what family fun was all about, what was? The cute little FourPlay, on the needlessly hysterical advice of Chundle's legal counsel, never made it into series production. But the lesson that families who play together stay together—right up to the last sickening instant—was stamped on the minds and the bodies of every family ever lured into taking a spin.

Sir-5-R 1957

Maybe, as the industry's most eminent spokesmen so eloquently whined, safety didn't sell in 1957. But safety—or the lack of it—was becoming an image albatross nonetheless, with dead people's families refusing to let bygones be bygones. Matterhorn Motors' solution: the Safe-T-Matic safety dream car, a four-ton rolling fortress bristling with anti-crash defenses. The car had just been completed when Matterhorn management had second thoughts. Whoa! Wouldn't it beg the question of why Matterhorn's production cars were such death traps? Cranks would start asking why

Matterhorn wasn't putting those true safety advances on the road. So, it was hold back on progress. Thus did the Safe-T-Matic become the Sir-5-R, a name so cryptic that most people wouldn't even know what it meant. Painstaking retro-engineering reduced safety claims to 12 percent brighter brake light bulbs and a louder horn. Then, further insights: The image of that huge orange hulk would only depress thrill-seeking auto-show visitors, so keep it under wraps. Better yet, send it to the crusher. The car that doesn't exist is the safest car of all.

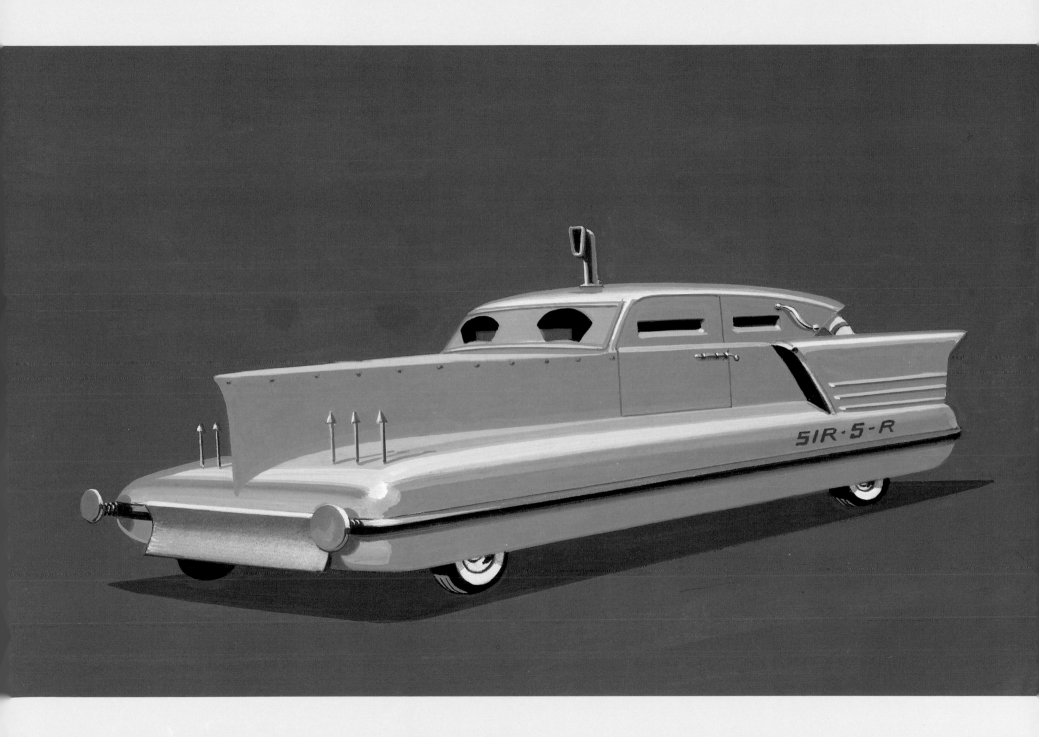

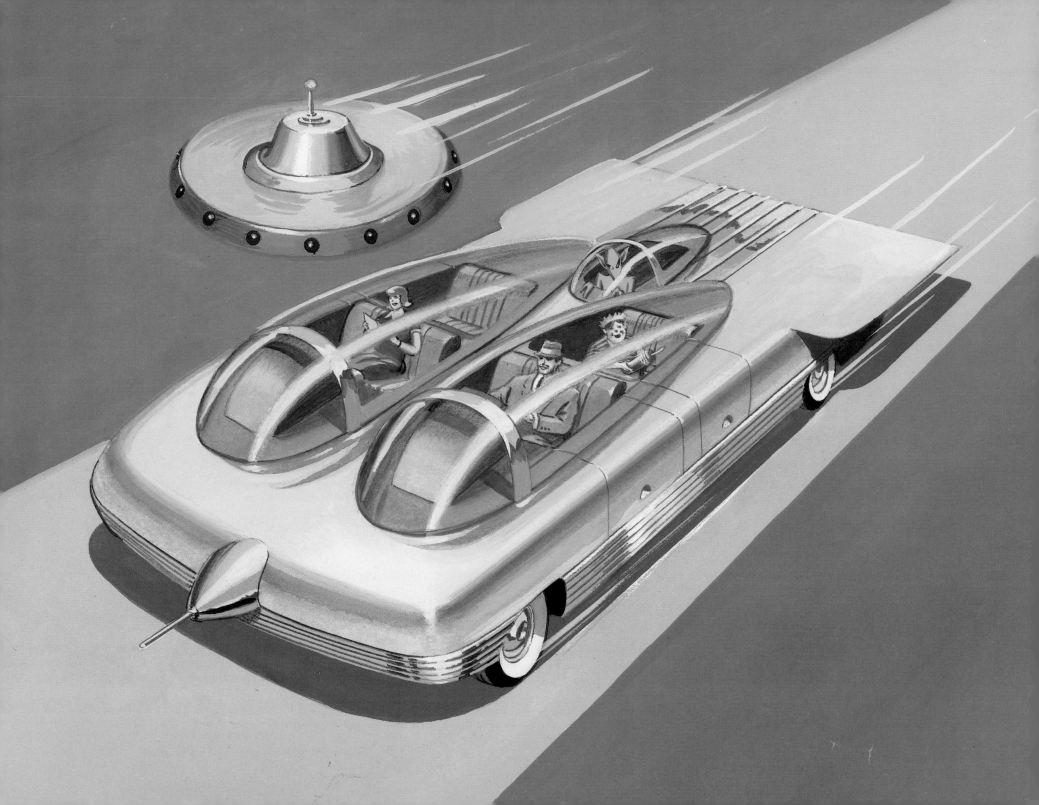

Orbitronic Minus-Zero Saucersnatcher, 1956

Sealed into their twin pressurized Plexi-Domes, the vigilant American family needn't breathe fresh air or get out of their seats for days as the Orbitronic, with its 400-gallon fuel tank, roamed the highways and byways of the great Southwest in search of flying saucers. America had lathered itself into even more fear and frenzy than usual since the first saucers were reported back in 1947. Those dipsy-doodling interlopers from another world, likely manned by Venusian Communists or Martian fellow-travelers, were clearly up to no good or they'd have long since surrendered to the authorities or landed on the White House lawn and asked to join NATO or SEATO. The Orbitronic's mission: Track 'em, so U.S. Air Force interceptors could attack 'em. Then get to the wreck to apprehend survivors. With its airtight built-in rear Isolation Dome for carrying a captured space creep to the nearest hoosegow, the Saucersnatcher was a dream car made for both patriotism and family fun. Amphetamine "pep pills" would keep Dad hyper-alert and super-energetic behind the wheel for weeks, while Mom dished out "space meals" of artificial meat-loaf nuggets and Junior and Sis scanned the heavens for a glimpse of another extraterrestial invader. Orbitronic: another way of saying "America on Guard."

Kooler Korporal VFW Post #423, 1958

Now, here's an oddity: a Veterans of the Foreign Wars post that's also a dream car, and a dream car that's also America's fastest beer truck. Credit Monolith Motors' Hamtramck, Michigan, UAW axle plant steward for the idea of honoring our overseas war vets with their own fantasy four-wheeler—that's him in the picture, ever-present ice-cold brewski in hand. "Sergeant Al" had seen the horror of thirst-crazed VFW buddies at picnics, cut off from their line of beer supplies and so parched of throat that the dirty jokes dried up to a few feeble croaks. If Monolith Motors could see its way clear to remedying the tragedy with a fast, maneuverable beer wagon, UAW Branch 32 might in turn see its way clear not to go out on strike next month and screw the company's profit for the quarter (a symbol of that American knack for the kind of compromise that makes both sides winners). The deal was done. The Kooler Korporal soon embarked on its Michigan-wide tour of VFW installations. VFW Post #422 would be forced to sell Post #423 within the year in a financial emergency that had threatened to leave it without funds for the big annual Xmas Eve stag smoker, and the UAW would strike the axle plant regardless of the original pact. The freedom to break a promise—wasn't that what Sergeant Al and his buddies had fought for?

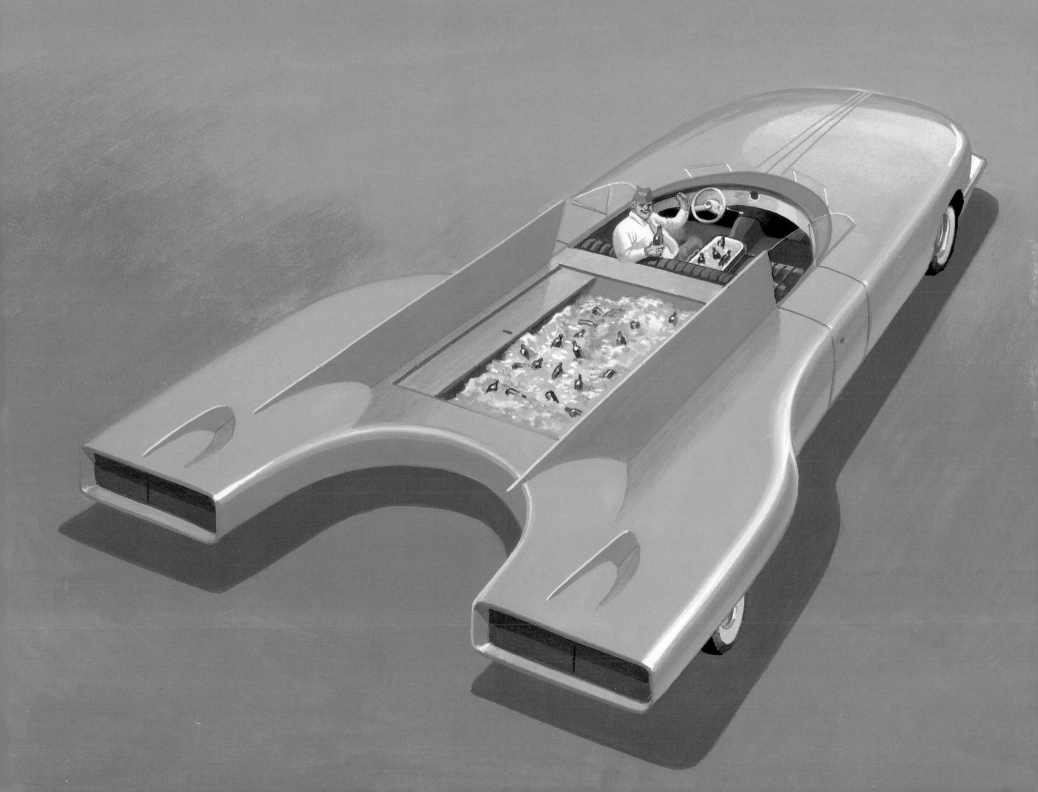

Nixoneer Squelchoramic RN, 1959

Vice President Richard M. Nixon's 1959 Moscow "kitchen debate" with Soviet bossman Khrushchev had repercussions that quickly rippled all the way to Mastodon Motors' Detroit dream-car skunk works. Feeling even more humiliated and mocked than usual, the angry Veep ordered Mastodon to ready an all-American riposte to shut up his Commie tormentor for good in any follow-up fracas. The Nixoneer Squelchoramic, designed and built in one feverish weekend, was more than just a stylish full-size Detroit luxury chariot. It was a dream car so true to the American dream that it carried a veritable panoply of electric domestic labor-saving devices—fridge, oven, washer-dryer, dishwasher, sink, and hi-fi record player. Moreover, it carried them on the *outside,* for all the free world to share. Only in America. And only from the genius of American industry. Khrushchev's imminent U.S. visit would afford the pretext for a return engagement where Mr. Nixon could squelch his loudmouthed Soviet tormentor for good. Leaving nothing to chance, he arrived the night before at Mastodon's skunk works to check out the Nixoneer's controls. The Vice President had never been famed for his manual dexterity; Mastodon technicians cowered and blanched as he pushed, pulled, and punched until every appliance was jammed or busted. The showdown was scrubbed, and Mastodon Motors remained on the Nixon Enemies List until long after the Cold War was over.

Brainstar Space Lab Silver Satellite, 1958

Sputnik's shocking 1957 success meant one thing to a stunned America: If even the stumblebum Russian Communists could turn out scientists smart enough to reach outer space, American kids were morons. Blackstone Corp. was quick to come up with a fix: the mobile classroom-lab-observatory called the Brainstar. Every real American family would *have* to have one, to lock the young 'uns inside and keep driving around until they'd cracked the riddle of launching a U.S. satellite capable of bumping *Sputnik* out of its orbit and reclaiming the heavens for God, the American Way, and enslaved peoples everywhere except in friendly Central American dictatorships. Thanks to their incarceration in the educational Brainstar, in a year—two at the outside—the little jerks would be smart enough to bail the nation out of its post-*Sputnik* funk and get back to watching Lawrence Welk. It was an idea whose time had come, the Brainstar. Too bad Blackstone couldn't get the government to pay for its development and had to quickly fold the program. Private enterprise, throttled by the Washington bureaucrats—again.

Italio Rapscalio Tipo 98.8 La Strada, 1954

Detroit's response to the cachet and excitement of foreign-built sports cars in the early Fifties is epitomized by the dramatic La Strada, combining sporty nomenclature with traditional American size, weight, chrome, fuel thirst, whitewalls, and room for a family of four to go racing against those upstart Continental puddle jumpers. Even ascot-wearing imported-car snobs agreed that a four-seat racer took the cake—Mom, Sis, and Junior holding on for dear life as Dad dueled with professional daredevils on dangerous road circuits in a U.S.-European grudge race to the death. Maintaining traditional American standards of comfort, luxury, and conve-nience in an all-out road racer was no problem for the La Strada's ingenious designers: They built it on the regular Bulgemobile Roadblaster Boulevardier Club Limousine sedan chassis for that patented "Whipped-Cream Ride," built in quick-opening passenger barf bags, and added a can of adhesive ban-dages to the glove box. It was the extra weight of just such safety advances, a spokesperson explained, that slowed the La Strada's speed to what the pros term "a crawl" and kept it from ever entering a race. But if there were ever a race with those reckless foreign hotheads for the finest four-place family sports car ever designed, the La Strada would have won hands-down.

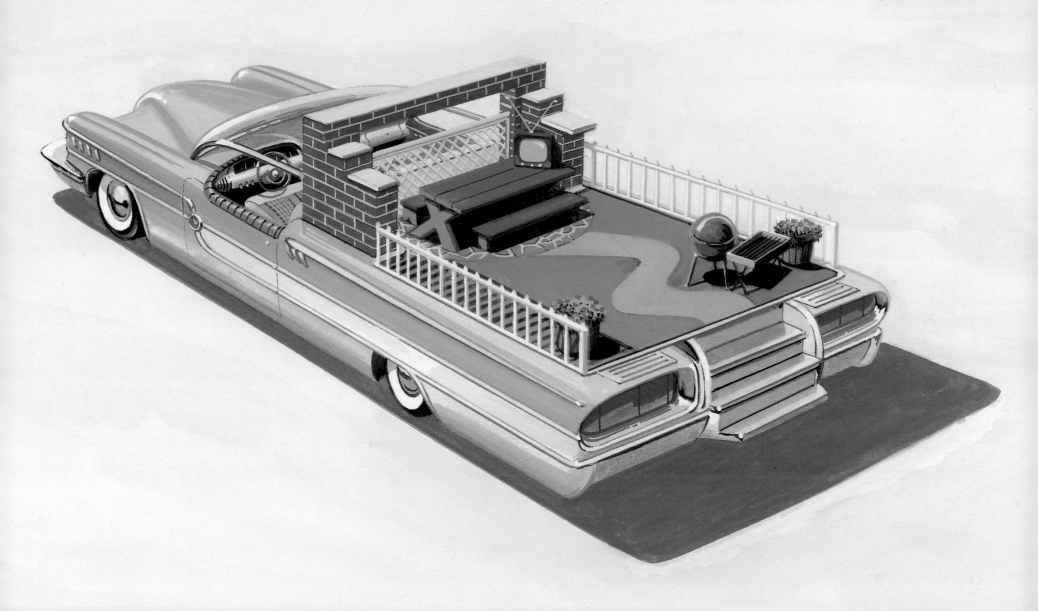

Bar-B-King Royal Patio Leisureliner, 1955

From *Rebel Without a Cause* to what Cheryl Crane did to her mom's boyfriend Johnny Stompanato that night in L.A., family fun *was* the Fifties. So the Bar-B-King Royal Patio Leisureliner, with its fully retractable all-American backyard on wheels, was an all but inevitable dream-car brainstorm. Here was outdoors family life at 55 miles per hour—picnic table, TV, barbecue grill, potted plants, and all the fixins, the entire flagstoned shebang automatically folding up and stowing itself away at the first sign of rain. But if the idea was right for the times, the technology seemed to lag slightly behind them. Matterhorn Motors engi-neers could bear the auto-show boos when their complex retracting mech-anism unfailingly shuddered and jammed midway through its gyrations. But when a routine demonstration at the New York Auto Show turned to horror, and all three TV networks kept a forty-two-hour vigil while res-cuers searched for the Matterhorn spokesbabe trapped deep inside the machinery, Matterhorn management had had enough. Bar-B-King Royal Patio Leisureliner Mk II featured a trunk-mounted picnic basket, two col-lapsible stools, and no moving parts.

La Niagara Ne Plus Ultrachic, 1959

The opening of the St. Lawrence Seaway in 1959 marked a watershed of progress in North American commerce. Oceangoing ships could now ply the waters from the Atlantic all the way to the end of the Great Lakes, halfway across the continent. That was enough for Matterhorn Motors' dream merchants: They presented the La Niagara Ne Plus Ultrachic, both honoring and glamorizing the Seaway. Niagara Falls was near it, after all, and that spectacular tourist site inspired the even more spectacular idea of an *actual waterfall* cascading over the rear deck of a sleek hardtop coupe. Water laced with detergent for that realistic foamy, bubbling effect was constantly recirculated from a fifty-gallon tank in the trunk—and though the La Niagara's occupants couldn't quite see the man-made wonder, they could watch following traffic scramble to avoid the wake of windblown soap foam constantly swirling behind, cars that spinned and skidded as those billions of greasy droplets slicked down the road. The La Niagara was replaced the following season by the even more daring La Tropicana, in which an oversized glass tank swarming with live tropical fish was substituted for the waterfall (and the trunk). It was intriguing, dream-car fanciers agreed, but it just wasn't the same.

Fin-Landia Choiceflow Fundeck, 1959

Your very own twenty-piece set of designer-certified tail fins, made to be snapped into place as you chose in pre-cut slots on the car's rear deck: Was this a halcyon era for America's discriminating car buyers, or what? The raw truth beneath the ingenious Fin-Landia was, alas, less sunny. By 1959 the tail fin craze was fading fast and Blackstone Motors' styling savants had no new gimmick up their sleeves. When the Fin-Landia inspiration struck, it symbolized both creativity and desperation. Auto-show audiences were briefly wowed by the novelty of a homemade, personalized styling statement. But by the time Blackstone could tool up to turn the dream car into a showroom version, fins were finally finis. The hastily produced Fin-Landia arrived on the market as the answer to a question nobody had asked. Ironically, an intact twenty-piece set of mint Choiceflow Fundeck tail fins has recently fetched as much as two hundred dollars on the eBay Internet auction block, proving that there's gold in them thar flops.

Cuba Libre 1, 1959; Cuba Libre 2, 1960

What inspires Americans more than a tiny nation rising up against oppression and forcing a despot to flee? Thus did Cuba's 1959 Revolution, which toppled the corrupt and brutal Batista regime, call for its Yanqui neighbor's plaudits—and, tribute of tributes, the fabulous Cuba Libre dream car, as lush and exciting and colorful as that Caribbean jewel itself. Auto showgoers flocked to see this symbol of hope for all enshackled folk everywhere and agreed that Bulgemobile's styling Svengalis had captured the spirit of Cuba Libre down to the last chrome spear-sweep and roll of pleated baby-alligator seat upholstery. But nothing inspires righteous American wrath more than an ingrate double-crossing greaser who steers his ramshackle banana republic into the hell of Red Russian–style Communism. So a year later, when bearded strongman Castro thumbed his nose at Uncle Sam and everything he stands for, Bulgemobile's immediate answer was Cuba Libre II, a four-wheeled prayer for the liberation of a captive nation. It was the original Cuba Libre stripped down, beat up, cheapened, and made as crummy as Communistic Cuba itself. Auto showgoers flocked to the stand again, this time to jeer with an all-American razzberry that the cigar-smoking bully couldn't fail to miss. If Cuba Libre II was a disgrace to the glory of the dream car and an affront to the idea of the automobile itself, so be it. A shot in the foot still counts as a blow against tyranny. Doesn't it?

Bumsmobile Gold Rush Xpress, 1958

Autodom took its first swing ever at honoring the national pastime with this eye-catching dream-car creation by Mammoth Motors, timed to coincide with the epochal shift of the Brooklyn Dodgers franchise to Los Angeles. The Bumsmobile could carry the complete equipment of a major-league ball club in its rear Dugout Cargo Deck and nine ball-players in its three rows of seats. Built-in spittoons accommodated tobacco-chewers, and that big blue L.A. Dodgers cap was designed to electrically tip itself, like a home-run hitter acknowledging an ovation, whenever a hidden electric eye detected a pretty gal. Mammoth flacks decided to kick off the Bumsmobile's public career with a gala "celebration drive" from Brooklyn to L.A. after the last-ever game at historic Ebbets Field in October of 1958. Doubtless intrigued by this sleek new wonder-mobile, excited longtime Dodger partisans surrounded it as it departed for the Far West. Eyewitnesses later testified that by the time it reached the Brooklyn Bridge, its admirers formed a seething mob, howling fare-well and godspeed, or something. That it never reached the bridge's other end became both an enduring mystery and another enduring piece of Dodgers lore.

Silver Magyar FunTrak Freedom Fighter Mk 56

Here's a dream car with attitude! Call this half family-holiday luxury coupe, half medium tank a rolling, rousing "Amen!" to the U.S. Government's two-fisted war of words in support of Hungary's heroic if abortive 1956 uprising. Seamlessly blending a spirit of pure bellicosity with elegant "Warflair" styling, Blackstone Motors' tracked and turreted dream machine took a bloody Cold War tragedy and made it fun for the whole family. The Silver Magyar wasn't called a freedom fighter for nothing: Included in its design were freedom to enjoy fiery Molotov cocktail V-8 power, freedom to bask in the radio's advanced Zithermatic Sound—with live shortwave broadcasts of the Hungarian heroes' desperate pleas for help just a finger touch away—and best of all, freedom to feel lucky to be an American. Our government's savvy policy of urging the Hungarians to revolt and then turning its back when they did taught a vital lesson in self-reliance that they have vowed to never forget. As for the Silver Magyar FunTrak Freedom Fighter Mk 56, Hungarian visitors to the Blackstone Motors Dream Museum demolished it in 1991 in a spontaneous orgy of enthusiasm. Nuff sed!

JetStar Super Athabaskan Premiere, 1957

What had American car fans been clamoring for, if not an indoor swimming pool on wheels that drained out in minutes to become a mobile billiards room that with ingenious Flip-Floor GyroSwing Action turned into a sandbox big enough for a Cub Scout pack? Something else, as it transpired—anything else, judging by the apathy with which auto showgoers greeted Mastodon Motors' feature dream car of the 1957 season. Critics theorized that the Athabaskan flouted the high-concept principle of all successful dream cars: one clear idea, easily grasped. If so—if it erred by giving people too much to think about at the same time, and showgoers after all were already burdened by having to remember where their cars were parked and which pocket their wallets were in—this should have come as no surprise. The Athabaskan was the spawn of a Mastodon economy drive that forced three dream-car concepts into a single vehicle. And a stock Mastodon station wagon, at that. As dream cars go, the Athabaskan went nowhere, yet the company failed to heed the lesson failure taught. For 1958, its Vortex DareSweep Gigolo Bilbao dream car combined a four-door hardtop with a two-seat roadster with a pickup truck.

Pontefract Golden Alligator Royal Mastodon Mk 9 Limolette, 1958

"Lady Lumberjack" flannel interior fabrics in a choice of black-and-red or red-and-black checks . . . BearTronic Eye, sounding a simulated grizzly growl on detecting any ursine creature within fifty feet . . . a fold-out all-aluminum Highway Hammock. That was the Golden Alligator, a go-anywhere, do-nothing, come-back-home exercise in three-tone paint and anodized gold accents that typified the Fifties fascination with overstatement for its own sake. Pontefract Division of Matterhorn Motors had proven a past master of this exotic dream-car genre. For example, a sensa-

tion of the '54 auto-show circuit was its Snoberie El Chic Landau Supreme, a car so exclusive that there was room only for the driver, yet without doors even for him or her—and sans headlights as well, since they were a feature found on the most common automobiles. Indeed, no Pontefract dream car would ever fall into the trap of practicality, and a popular game among auto-show regulars was to bet among themselves on the purpose of the latest gleaming Pontefract dream of . . . what?

Cremeliner Country Cousin, 1955

"Hey, Pop, can I have the keys to the Cremeliner?" Next to "I'm telling the House Un-American Activities Committee on you," that must have been America's most commonly heard phrase back in 1955. Advanced? The Cremeliner's simulated knotty-pine interior paneling was 100 percent spruce-scented. And how's about that HiWay HiBall push-button pop-up wet bar? Somebody say "Hic Transit Gloria"? Bulgemobile Corp.'s stylists didn't know it at the time, but the Cremeliner was a four-wheeled letter of intent promising motordom that the sport-utility vehicle was on its way. Forty-five years ago, in Cremeliner form, it was still a cloud no bigger than a cumulonimbus—but at four and a half tons, with its buckboard ride, trucklike comfort, ravenous fuel thirst, and boxcar dimensions that made parking a cross between a demolition derby and a sentence of hard labor, the Cremeliner had defined the shape of things to come.

Ticonderoga Custom El Mocambo, 1958

Who'd ever want to step outside, when the Ticonderoga's split-level Living Center offered the three-in-one recreational bonanza of a horseshoe pitch, a shuffleboard court, and ten-pin bowling? Meanwhile, that powerful roof-mounted, color-keyed telescope could spot the next drive-in restaurant from three miles away. And how Mom loved ChoreMatic, the rear bench seat that flipped over to become a road-going ironing board! Mastodon Motors pulled out all the stops with this ultimate station wagon, so attuned to the times that fuel consumption was precisely synchronized with the distance between gas stations along the brand-new Interstate Highway System—so the Ticonderoga family-on-the-go could stop at every one. Other firsts included Fishbowl Visiglass, ground to actually *magnify* the world outside for a startling close-up effect, and a breakthrough BladderMatic Eye to detect running water, telltale sign of a working bathroom, up to half an hour away.

Golden Guitar Twangstar Coupe de Pompadour, 1957

What crazy hepcats called rock and roll had penetrated all the way to the Motor City by 1957, when Mastodon Motors contracted with the bobby-soxers' swivel-hipped idol himself, Elvis Presley, for exclusive rights to a dream car honoring the sorghum-voiced backwoods balladeer and his hot rhythm combo. Mastodon stylists were unable to decipher the tieless crooner's own sketches, on peanut-butter-and-banana-smeared prescription blanks. A panel of top radio disc jockeys, consulted for their expertise on teen tastes, mysteriously quit en masse after Mastodon answered their demand to be paid in drugs and partying with bottles of aspirin and square-dance invitations. Appeals for help never reached the Elvis Presley Fan Club, which seemed to move trailer camps every week. The stylists gave up and threw together a mishmash of tasteless decoration, loud colors, and such vulgar excesses as a life-size chromed head of Mr. Presley for the hood ornament—a parody of the rude, crude rock and roll style. The Golden Guitar Twangstar was a smash auto-show sensation from day one. Those hepcats really dug that real gone look. And "Elvis the Pelvis" showed every indication of one day rivaling the popularity of the Old Groaner, Bing Crosby, himself.

HobbyPop RoadShop, 1956

C'mon, Mom, drive smoother—Dad's trying to build a birdhouse downstairs! It was a fat slice of pure Fifties lifestyle on wheels: the Little Lady safely out of the way at her chores while Hubby does whatever he feels like. What American male didn't need a hobby or two, to let off all the steam built up trying to teach his lovable birdbrain how to balance a checkbook or waiting for that martini she should have mixed an hour ago? And the RoadShop was a rolling hobby hacienda for the man of the house. Matterhorn Motors' dream-designers didn't stint. Down there in the RoadShop was a man's-man's world of band saws, fretsaws, buzz saws, jigsaws, and sawtooth files, enough to keep the Big Guy busy from Toledo to Tuscaloosa fussing over that new pipe rack or cribbage board—well-deserved gifts by himself, to himself. He might let the Ball and Chain into his lair sometimes, sure, but only to clean up or take down a snack order. She does love serving her man! So gobble down a few more pep pills, Mom, and let's not hear any more of that back talk. You're going to be pulling another all-nighter behind the wheel!

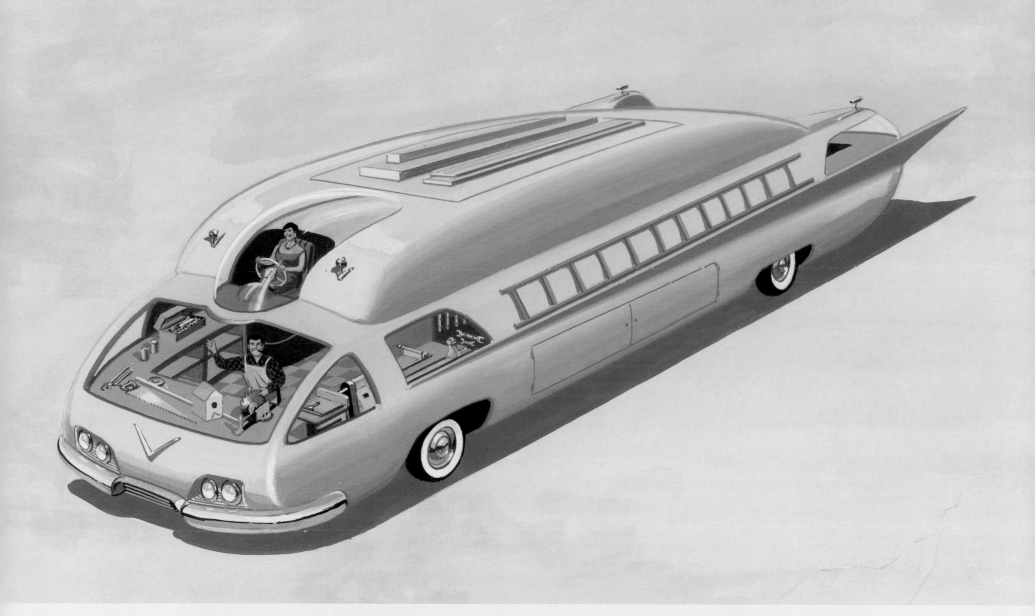

Monte Cristo Skyliter DeThrille, 1958

Sweepflyte Motion, harnessing the invisible power of gravity to keep all four wheels glued to the road, was easy to overlook among the sleekly bustle-backed Monte Cristo's bulging grab bag of advanced new claims. How about Quadra-Flote Pillo-Plus Engineering—every tire *rolling on a cushion of air?* And for luxury connoisseurs, the auto-show spokesbabe trilled, there was HumanTuch Magic Ignition, to ensure that the car wouldn't start before the driver personally turned the key. It was features such as these that excited 1958 Chicago Auto Show opening-day spectators by the thousands to rush headlong to the next exhibit, and led Blackstone Motors publicists to overhaul their Monte Cristo spiel overnight. Gone the next day, in fact, was any spiel at all—only a pencil-beam spotlight trained on a stripper where yesterday a car had been. It didn't have anything to do with the quest for automotive creativity and excellence, the fuddy-duddies grumbled; but then, as a spokesman explained, neither did the Monte Cristo. Touché.

Bard-Oh Ooh-La-La Femme Fatale, 1955

With its gynecologist-approved Sex Kitten styling, silk lingerie floor mats, and retractable "Bikinitop," the Ooh-La-La was Pontefract Motors stylists' response to the challenge thrown down by their company's chairman one day at the nineteenth hole of a posh suburban Detroit country club: "Say, what if that Brigitte Bardot doll were a *car?*" The outcome uncannily captured the essence of the pouty Gallic sexsation, with what press releases described as "sophistication equal to race day at the Moulin Rouge, plus all the romance of the Eiffel Tower bathed in Riviera moonlight."

Authentic French touches included dual roof-mounted baguette racks and twin pre-emptied deodorant spray cans, and the Ooh-La-La even ran on specially formulated perfume-scented gasoline. La Bardot's reported suicide threat within days of the car's debut was dismissed as a mere publicity ploy and not a criticism of this American *homage,* and in any event failed to prevent the Ooh-La-La from taking Sexiest Newcomer honors at the 1955 Cannes Film Festival.

Armageddon Mk 1, 1958

It was every American family's Fifties dream—a fallout shelter on wheels. Blending top-down open-road driving adventure with the safety of a foot-thick antiradiation shield and enough canned bologna in its capacious trunk to feed the whole gang long after friends and neighbors had all starved to death! Versatility? The Armageddon drove and rode like the purebred family sports tank it was, a symphony in reinforced, lead-lined concrete with more sizzle 'n' snap under the hood than an A-bomb at a cookout. But let the sirens start wailing and the sky turn purple and a hot wind blow in from hell, and it's everybody down that airtight hatch on the double, where Dad takes over the dual downstairs controls, Mom breaks out the antinausea pills, and Sis and Junior man the gunports, poised to blow the head off anybody trying to cadge a ride. They might never drop the Big One smack on Maple City—but what a thrill to imagine driving through a devastated nuclear wasteland in the comfort, safety, and luxury of the Armageddon Mk 1. So thanks, Blackstone Motors, for gifting the Fifties with a whole new bold all-American dream!

Russbuster Bearbait Showdowner, 1959

"Hey, Ivan," this simulated family tankbuster seemed to say, "let's play Who Blinks First!" Bulgemobile stylists imagined the ultimate Cold War confrontation as the Russbuster's starting point: Mr. and Mrs. Average U.S. Citizen, out for a Sunday drive after church with Junior and Sis, happen upon a godless Communist Soviet Red Army patrol blocking the intersection of Main Street and Jones Avenue. After all, what with fluoridated drinking water and other takeovers straight out of Moscow's playbook already eroding Americans' freedoms, it *could* happen here. But one look at the Russbuster, bristling with nonauthentic styling advances that seemed to threaten awesome firepower while laughing off direct shell hits, and the big bad Russkie bear would be hightailing it back to his lair faster than you could say "Don't forget your balalaika!" A dream car with a chip on its shoulder—just the kind of morale-builder Mr. and Mrs. U.S. Citizen needed back in those Cold War times. But now turn the Russbuster around, Dad. Over there! Junior just spotted a peacenik!

Burning Foot Double Bogey Green Eagle, 1959

If folks insisted on walking, what was the point of the dream car? That insight spawned the Burning Foot, swelling the primitive concept of the golf cart up to limousine levels of luxury while extending the smooth, soft, sedentary lifestyle of the Fifties to the links. Forget physical exertion, that was for Commie peasants. Powering around the course with the divot-digging acceleration of its 400-horsepower Pow-R-Stroke V-8, the Burning Foot let you play eighteen holes in twelve minutes. Talk about speeding up the game! And from your armchair perch in that air-conditioned rear clubhouse, *every* hole was a nineteenth hole. Trading the tedium of exercise and mental concentration for a whole new rhythm of swing-sit-drink-bet-drink, swing-sit-drink-bet-drink was as in tune with the Fifties as the three-martini lunch. Of course, with the Burning Foot abroad on the fairways, "Fore!" would come to mean "Run for your life!" And golf courses would have to trade their old-fashioned grass for asphalt if this dream machine were to ever become reality. But why should those few acres of green be treated any different anyway, in a nation so bent on paving itself over from sea to shining sea?

MomChore RoadDrudge XXX, 1958

Wait a minute, Matterhorn Motors' dream-car alchemists exclaimed. If we can whip up a HobbyPop RoadShop for dads, surely we can cook up something special for the distaff side! And did they ever! The MomChore RoadDrudge copped *Happy Home* magazine's coveted Stamp of Satisfaction the same day the first ad ran in *Happy Home*—'cause here was a decorator-approved Fifties paradise-on-wheels that put the American hausfrau behind the wheel, the stove, the ironing board, the sewing and washing machines, *and* the dirty dishes while her lovable lug browsed the sports pages back in the off-limits Leisure Pit, waiting for his ham sandwich. What a waste of time for a homemaker to just sit there soaking up the scenery! And anyway, why should the cooking and baking and sewing and ironing and darning chores pile up just because the domestic Jill-of-all-trades wasn't at her post back home? But here's an oddity: Housewives claimed to *hate* the MomChore RoadDrudge, and at the 1958 Kansas City Garage and Kitchen Exposition an all-gal human battering ram literally knocked it off its pedestal! The wrong flowers in those cunning little planters, perhaps, or something about the curtain arrangement. Maybe some of the all-male Matterhorn dream-car team should have asked the better half for tips on how to please their fickle sisters? But heck, do something like that and the little cupcakes might start getting ideas. And that would have ruined everything the Fifties stood for!

Stratoblaster SAC LeMay, 1958

The Stratoblaster was meant to do on the new U.S. Interstate Highway System what the mighty bomber armada of the Strategic Air Command did in the skies: stay ever-ready to react at any moment to any threat. For the SAC, Red Soviet Russian attack. For the Stratoblaster, the kind of lane-clogging, traffic-snarling, slow-moving roadhog who makes any true American's blood run red. Most of them the elderly, the infirm, the timid, sure—but all of 'em doing the dirty work of Soviet saboteurs: Those inter-state dawdlers could be holding up troop transports, military cargoes, SAC General Curtis E. LeMay himself on this road system built to ensure fast long-distance transport in case of atomic war. Kudos to Mastodon Motors for detecting yet another menace to peace of mind in those fear-filled Fifties. And for mixing dream car and dream weapon in the overpowered, oversized, overweight Stratoblaster, fast and massive enough to chase down any witless dupe of the Commie conspiracy and bunt him into the weeds. "Overkill," whimpered left-wing egghead pantywaists—this was vigilante justice unleashed on the innocent. Didn't those poor parlor pinkos get it? In the Fifties climate of proud patriotic paranoia that produced the Stratoblaster, the innocent were the most suspect of all!

Conformoramic SuperSheep Anonybus, 1956

Its Flannel Gray finish was real gray flannel. Every occupant sat sealed off from every other occupant in his own cubicle, the juniormost taking up the rear. The president, or driver, could "fire" any passenger at will, simply by stopping and ordering him out. It was corporate life on wheels! If the Fifties white-collar yes-man in the gray flannel suit was a hero for his times, what did that make the Conformoramic SuperSheep Anonybus? More than just a shuttle bus for company execs! Anonybus riders got the company house organ to read, a PA system blaring nonstop company news and rules, and the company song for sing-alongs—even complimentary preprinted, prestamped postcards, complimenting the boss on a job well done. Any career-savvy human corporate cog who knew what was good for him would *beg* to ride the Anonybus. One obviously disgruntled off-duty New York showgoer in gray flannel did go berserk at the sight of the Conformoramic and attacked it with his briefcase. Another soreheaded non–team player in a business suit committed suicide by impaling himself on its skyscraper-shaped hood ornament. His widow apologized to his boss, and though she didn't get the pension she was after, she at least received a complimentary copy of the company's annual report. (Thanks to team play and wise leadership, profits were up.)

Hula Hoopster, 1957

World peace, racial amity, alleviation of poverty—important, you bet. But the art of rotating plastic rings around the pelvis while standing in place was the kind of challenge Americans rose to in the Fifties with that Yankee do-or-die spirit. And it was Chundle Motors that beat the industry to the auto shows in 1957 with a dream car spun around the Hula Hoop. Showgoers of all ages ached to jump into the Hula Hoopster's padded Hula-torium and start gyrating themselves dizzy. Amid all the fun, how could Chundle's fantasy fabricators have known that the combination of a moving car and Hula-Hooping boggled the human system to the brink, then right over it, of digestive distress? They found out when their brainchild embarked on its national cross-country "Hello Hula Hoopster Holiday on Asphalt" goodwill tour. Or more precisely, whenever another queasy-faced kid staggered away after a stint in the Hula-torium. A debacle? Anything but! The miracle of washable automobile upholstery was an advance that, but for the Hula Hoopster, might not have arrived for years.

Bongo Beatnik Ferlinghetti TurboHipster, 1959

Stung by accusations that Fifties Detroit was "out of it," culture-wise, Monolith Motors hit upon a dream-car idea that would put the snobs and crypto-sophisticates in their place but good. Detroit, out of the loop? Take *this,* all you mopey longhairs! The black-on-black Bongo Beatnik Ferlinghetti TurboHipster not only incorporated a working espresso bar, French café furniture, all-wax-candle interior lighting, and a rear height-adjustable Poetronic Recital Pod. Those were only surface touches. It also drove *only in circles,* to symbolize the futility of life's journey. Overhead spigots drizzled a constant rainlike mist, to further depress the occupants.

And the lack of a fuel tank made an existential statement about man's essential helplessness in an uncaring and hostile universe. But the very Beats the Ferlinghetti was meant to impress shrugged off invitations to the kickoff wine and cheese party at Marin County's finest country club. By the time motormouth Beat "writer" Jack Kerouac turned down Monolith's five-hundred-dollar offer to drive it cross-country and write a series of ads, it was clear that Detroit's effort to embrace an alternative culture was doomed. Detroit would never make the same mistake again.

KOOKY COOL 'N' CRAZY CATS -- CAUTION!

Bongo Beatnik

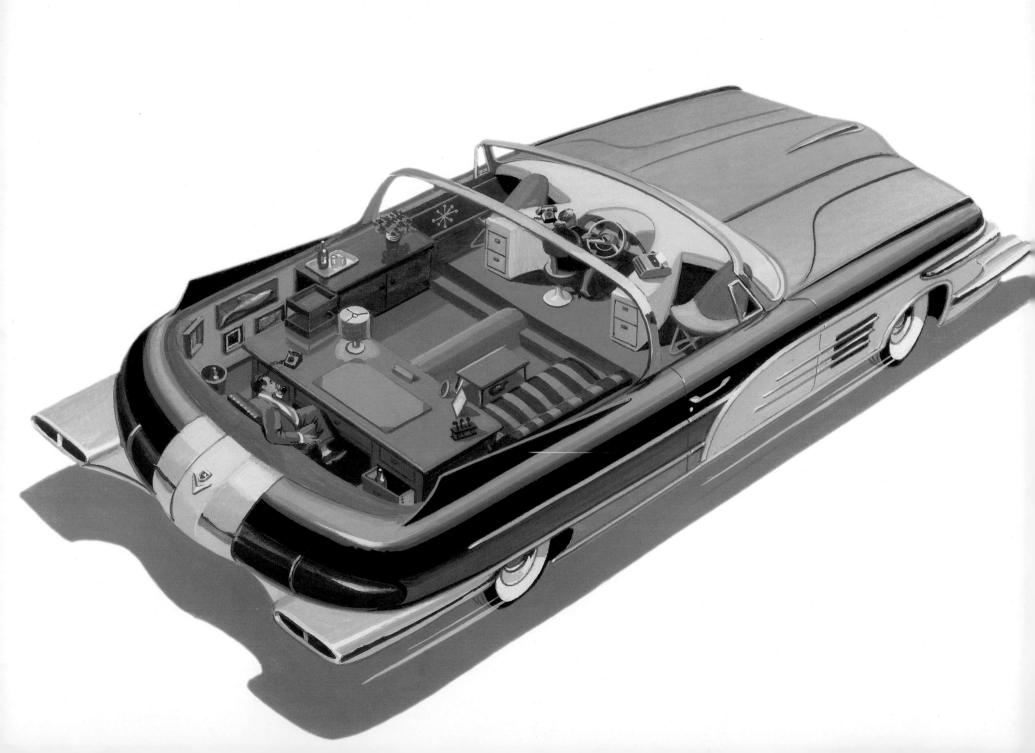

Bossmobile Gal Friday Execustreak, 1958

Bulgemobile Corp. decided to give the busy Fifties executive the break he needed with its premier dream car for the '58 season. Enter the fabulous Bossmobile, where the high-salaried corporate big shot could sit back, digest his three-martini lunch, and dictate memos or gab to his golf pro on the portable Electrofone or just uncap the Johnny Walker in the lower right-hand desk drawer for a bracing nip or three before the Bossmobile deposited him at his split-level suburban home in time for cocktail hour. Meanwhile, up front in her super-efficient Officejet Work Module, his Gal Friday would putter about—typing, filing, answering the phone, arranging her boss's golf dates and dry-cleaning pickup. And, by the way, driving. In case Mr. Big wanted to stop en route to hit a few buckets' worth at the driving range, Gal Friday could stay at her place and do his expense reports or collect all the empty Scotch bottles or give the Bossmobile a good waxing. No goofing off now, Missy; serving the men who run this world is a full-time job!

Curbsider Foodhog El Automatico X-Cess, 1959

America's Fifties romance with drive-in eating was bound to produce a dream car—but who'd have expected anything as bold, as brash, as unabashedly greedy for junk food, junk food, and more junk food as the all-devouring Curbsider? This big-mouthed road glutton featured twin motorized high-speed conveyor belts running rearward from just above grille level, designed to shuttle drive-in comestibles into the cabin in seconds. Inside, lucky Curbsider occupants ate from a pop-up, car-width "Insta-Trough" that automatically dumped leftover wrappings and debris into another conveyor, to be regurgitated onto the curb by a trio of chrome "tongues" mounted within the grille itself. From the moment the order was delivered until the last half-eaten bun spewed out could take less than sixty seconds. The Fifties were all about famished families on the go in search of filling their faces fast and on the cheap—and the Curbsider Foodhog El Automatico was the dream car they deserved!

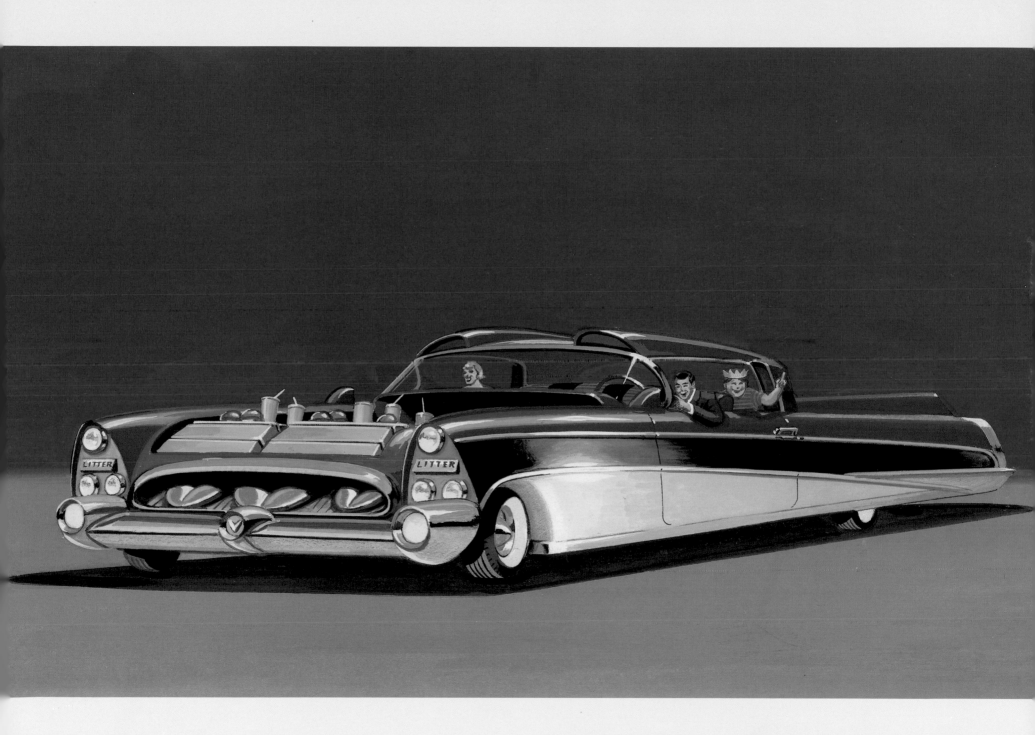

Fold-O-Matic Bonustar, 1959

Led by Volkswagen's ubiquitous Beetle, small-car sales were climbing so alarmingly as the Fifties came to a close that Detroit was forced—reluctantly—to act. Motor City moguls dismissed the small-car craze as a passing fad; American buyers would soon recover their senses and embrace the blundering, oversized gas-guzzler again. And unlike other Detroit makers sheepishly readying stripped-down compact models, Bulgemobile stunned the auto-show circuit in early 1959 with a dream car that not only refused to surrender to the smaller-is-better mania but showed you could have it both ways: the 32-foot-long Fold-O-Matic, three hefty tons of dyed-in-the-chrome Detroit extravagance—with a fold-away little puddle jumper tucked inside. In the unlikely event that the owner actually preferred to drive a sawed-off runt of a car, he could push a dashboard button and the trunk lid would rise, rails would extend to the road, and a series of sections would assemble themselves into a pint-sized demi-Bulgemobile ready to go. Take that, small-car faddists! Alas, Bulgemobile Corp.'s overweening pride in the classic American road blimp led to a last-minute decision not to reveal the tiny car huddled within the Fold-O-Matic's fat flanks. It was a decision to be regretted. When Tadaki Motors blatantly copied the same idea a few years later with its Kangaroo car-within-a-truck, Bulgemobile was unable to prove it had the idea first and lost its $400 million lawsuit.

Milltowner Happydaze, 1955

Virtually forgotten today is this, the only Detroit dream car designed to celebrate the introduction of the pharmaceutical miracle called Milltown and the onset of the Tranquilizer Age. It was not an uncontroversial gesture. Some averred that while such drugs might induce a state of mellow bliss in place of high anxiety, they also dulled the mind and blurred reality and . . . and whatever. Forgetfulness. Milltown might make you forget. But the Milltowner, what a wonderful terrific thing, to name a car after a tranquilizer. Is anybody reading this? What does it matter anyway? The smoothness and silence of the Milltowner made it feel as if you'd just taken a mouthful of pills. The smoothness and silence of the Milltowner. I want to lie down now. Haven't felt this rested in years. I could nod off right now. The smoothness and silence of the Milltowner. Wait a moment, did I already say that? Everything's so smooth and so easy, I could walk right out that . . .

NAME YOUR OWN DREAM CAR—THE DETROIT WAY!

Reproduced here for the first time ever by special permission of Bulgemobile Corp. is the long-secret official Bulgemobile 1959 Dream-Car Naming Guide! Now *you* can create an authentic Fifties Detroit dream-car name in seconds, just like Bulgemobile's own Department of Nomenclature did back in those fabulous days before meaning meant anything and when the names were as long as the cars!

Naming method #1:

Choose any line and, reading across, combine the words in Columns 1–2 and 3–4.

Naming method #2:

Choose any column and, reading down, combine the words on lines 1–2 and 3–4.

Naming method #3:

Close eyes and touch the page with your finger four times, moving your finger before each new touch.

1	2	3	4
Flash	Trak	Jet	Bolt
Power	Ray	Rocket	Sky
Blaze	Liner	Flair	Mark XX
Fire	Maxi-	Sabre	Quadra-
Blast	Sweep	Thrust	Storm
Dual	Stroke	Whirl-O-	Gale
Royal	Zest	Mono-	Hi-
Thrill	Flow	Silver	Path
Bomb	-Tronic	Finder	Wind
Crest	Streak	Mist	Dyno-
Cosmo	Astro	Smoke	Dream
Dare	Hawk	Sea	-Onic
Star	Strike	Land	Air
Wild	Roto	Phantom	Thunder
Golden	Flite	Flyte	-O-Matic

DREAM CARS

AROUND THE WORLD

It was as if the falling of the first domino had triggered a chain reaction that rippled around the world and into places where they didn't even play dominos: Detroit's invention of the dream car unleashed an energy force that carmakers from Europe to Asia were helpless to resist. The American example had proven that these daring four-wheeled imaginative leaps stirred car buyers the way Pavlov's experiments stirred dogs. But abroad, the more urgent motive was fear—fear that without similar automotive curiosities demonstrating their willingness to squander millions on cars never meant to be sold, non-American builders would come off as little better than a motley of behind-the-times cheapskates with a timid streak a kilometer wide.

That they *were* a motley of behind-the-times cheapskates with a timid streak a mile wide is neither here nor there. What matters is that by late 1957, a mere three years after the curtain went up on the first Cavalcade of Chrome at New York's Hotel Splendid-Fantastic, homemade European and Asian versions of this flamboyant American innovation were being unveiled on stages from London to Paris to Tokyo by carmakers determined to top the Americans at their own game.

It is easy in hindsight to fling about words like *flop* and *debacle* and *sheer lunacy.* What deserves to be remembered about those offshore dream cars and their public impact is that such words came equally easily forty years ago. European car fanciers, as became evident even before the Frenchmen among them went on spontaneous general strike outside the Auto Salon of the Potential Futures at the Palace of Brains in Paris in May 1958, dreamed differently than their American cousins. Indeed, the kind of automotive dream that turned the future-obsessed *Americaine* giddy seemed to translate into the Gallic word for *nightmare.* Car buyers in Great Britain and on the Continent alike were admittedly stimulated by exposure to the dream-car phenomenon—but, as auto industry analysts observed, stimulated mainly to cancel existing orders, stay clear of new-car showrooms, and place obscene or threatening phone calls to highly placed automotive executives for weeks following.

It was a far different story in the Far East. No sooner had the 1957 Tokyo Funhouse of Dreaming Wheels opened its doors than the Emperor himself composed a haiku, quickly interpreted by scholars as a lament against foolish woolgathering by *ki-chiha*—roughly translated as "men on wheels" or "fossil-fuel artisans." Published in the next day's issue of *Asahi Shinbun,* the haiku would impact Japan's emperor-worshiping populace like a royal proclamation. Funhouse of Dreaming Wheels attendance fell overnight from a crush of forty-two thousand to five Norwegian sailors and a freelance candied-worm vendor. The carmakers' ingenuity remained unaffected—one recalls Digatsu's 1959 Indoors Man, the only car of any kind designed exclusively for in-home driving—but Japanese dream cars were thereafter forced to masquerade at smaller venues as garden tools, sculptures by the handicapped, or movie props.

By the early 1960s, a fickle American public's unauthorized left turn into rationality, practicality, and, worst of all, common sense ushered in a new automotive era. The dream-car dream itself was over in Detroit, and soon around the globe. It would require a full three decades until carmakers and car buyers alike, once more riding high on confidence and fueled by an appetite for the bizarre and the flighty, rediscovered the pleasures of leaving their senses and dared to dive again into the realm of elaborate automotive fantasies with scant earthly purpose.

FRANCE

The French industry generated a flurry of dream cars between 1955 and 1960—intensely Gallic automotive visions, to the extent that an intellectual, a psychologist, and a government spokesperson were required to be on the display stand at motor shows to explain each car's philosophical and aesthetic underpinnings. Subtle and abstract at the same time, these French creations on the whole failed to convey a clear or even graspable idea or theme. The Canard firm's BX-38-976A-?, for example, carried not a driver's manual but a manifesto by its design team that linked the BX-38-976A-? to French Colonial policy in the postwar era and charged those blind to any connection between this and the car itself as "idiots, fools, and bourgeois materialists."

Shown at American exhibitions alongside their Detroit counterparts, the dream cars of France suffered, too, from the imposition of a two-franc (French currency only) viewing charge, the notorious "attention tax."

Of more than routine significance was the **Blois**

et Canard BD-177-XM, introduced at the Lille Auto Salon of January 1958. In the picture, a professor of thermodynamics delivers another of his hourly lectures on the passenger-heating properties of wool blankets. St. Tropez–based Blois et Canard had omitted a heating system from the BD-177-XM, but occupants in need of cooling down could grip a pipe that recirculated ice water from the wine cooler through the cabin floor.

The **Decliné** (pronounced "Dee-Clin-Ay") **Apocalypse** was technologically so far ahead of its time that not even its own designers knew for certain how to operate the pneumatic-hydraulic-electric-magnetic door locks—among myriad' innovations declared too good for the public and thus kept strictly confidential. The woman in the picture (opposite), relaxing offstage with a cigarette, is a former Decliné show mannequin and the

fifth wife of the firm's styling head. Her custom of hovering close to her husband's exhibits, and his show mannequins, endured almost as long as their marriage.

But the French and the dream car made, ultimately, an awkward match. The French dreamed in theories, with footnotes and a bibliography; such intellectual density proved to be a heavier load than any set of four wheels or brain cells was quite able to bear.

GREAT BRITAIN

The British motor industry, having done so little else other than dream for so many years, was ready. In spirit, at least; no car-making nation more eagerly embraced the chance to convert idle fantasy into automotive spectacle. That collective groans met so very many such efforts, and groans escalated all the way to the lamentable "Earls Court Riot" in London in October of 1955, had scant to do with creativity and everything to do with austerity. Yes, next to a three-dimensional triumph in metal and chrome and rubber, even a life-size, full-color cardboard cutout pales. But a disciplined frugality—or "mean, cheeseparing stinginess," to use English argot—had made multimillionaires and lords of many a jumped-up back-alley mechanic with a knack for cutting corners; and now, amid the workers' craze for decent wages and a turn of public fascination away from underpowered biscuit tins prone to stall in a heavy dew, the financial squeeze was on if Sunday polo at country houses was not to become a thing of the past. Thus, cardboard cutouts in lieu of the flashy American dream car.

The firm of Denbeigh & Sons' Successors Ltd. (1906) did eschew the fantasy-in-cardboard solution at London's Earls Court Motor Show in the fall of 1957. Denbeigh's **Flying Buttress** astonished showgoers, much of the hubbub emanating not so much from the car, a rather modest little bottle-nose saloon, as from the donation boxes studded about the stand. Denbeigh's solicited contributions to help allay the Flying Buttress's development costs, plus "something for a rainy day." To save the expense of trailering it back to the Midlands works, the car itself was offered as a raffle prize. Earls Court legend has it that no claimant ever stepped forward.

Of the concepts behind British dream cars over-all, little needs to be said beyond paying all due tribute to an industry so dependent on popular acceptance, so determinedly flouting it. "A Vacation Shooting Brake for Her Majesty the Queen, Wicker-Bodied." "A Gentleman's Weekend Lounging Coupe." "Commemorating the Relief of Mafeking in a Carry-All with Carved Ivory Friezes and Double Sandwich Hampers." The mind boggles, even if, in that otherwise green and sceptr'd isle, the dream of dream cars so quickly withered.

THE GERMANYS

"We do not dream, we think!" So spoke the chairman of the German Motor Vehicle Manufacturer's Consortium on behalf of the nation's major car companies in 1957, when they flatly declined to compete in lofting flights of automotive fancy. West Germany's carmakers went so far as to post notices in their factories forbidding employees to dream about cars but to report any dreams they did have, with sketches.

In the East, with so many hundreds of industrial exhibitions the nearest thing to popular entertainment, adapting the vulgar excesses of the perverted capitalist system to Socialist ideals was just the shot in the arm needed to boost attendance and glorify the DDR's heavy industry. Assigned in a bureaucratic mix-up to engineers experienced in the aircraft sector, the **Wartfunk JU-57 Sport Roadster** meant to kick off the program debuted at the 1958 Leipzig Iron Fair and was instantly hailed as a triumph of Marxist-Leninist-Ulbrichtian thought, albeit by its own manufacturer. Agreement was less than universal. Touring the Wartfunk exhibit on opening day, the East German Minister of Anti-Fascist Propaganda instantly recognized in this People's Dream Car more than a hint of a certain Nazi dive-bomber of the recent Great Patriotic War—and worse, that the boo-boo was officially his. Claiming that the abandoned brick factory housing the show had just suffered a sneak germ-warfare attack by hillbilly hooligans of the Yankee-led swine camp, he swiftly shut it down. Too late. East Germany's 1958 Miss Spirit of the Potash Quota Miracle had already posed for photos with the JU-57, photos splashed all over that day's bull-dog editions of the Party newspapers. A team of internal security investigators was already on the case. The credibility of the East German dream-car program was shot twenty-four hours after it had started, along with the Minister of Anti-Fascist Propaganda.

USSR

Communist Party Chairman N. Khrushchev's car-crazy playboy nephew Ricky crashed the 1956 Moscow May Day military parade to do wheelies in his Ferrari and was packed off to run the GUG truck factory in the Urals for his sins. Ricky was back in no time with the **GUG Red Dream** in tow.

He had personally plugged the Soviet Union's dream-car gap. And what a dream: samovar-fresh tea, tanklike ramming power, even rumble-seat exile for dissident passengers. The Red Dream was the talk of the Soviet exhibit at the 1958 Brussels World's Fair and might have brought a medal or two from a grateful Politburo. Incorrigible scape-grace Ricky scotched that when he defected, sold the car to the CIA as a Soviet secret weapon, and vanished with his cash-stuffed suitcase. The CIA, meanwhile, discovered the Red Dream to be nothing more than a solid block of papier-mâché and joined with the KGB in a manhunt that has never officially been called off.

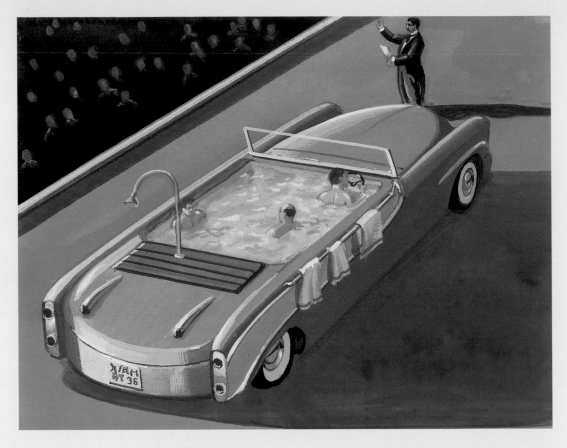

JAPAN

Language problems almost scuttled Japan's dream-car foray before it began. It was apparent at the 1957 Tokyo Gasoline and Diesel Congress, when dream cars named the Dirtysex, the Slutbitch Trollop, and the Whipster Moan so very briefly held the spotlight, that a mistranslation of *dream* had occurred. Nice dream intended, nasty dream tran-

scribed. Disaster proved to be deliverance in disguise: The chairmen of twelve car companies, octogenerians all, had lost face and resigned. The way was cleared for Young Turks of seventy and a fresh new Japanese industry leadership cadre.

One may quibble with their often inscrutable dream-car themes—and a creative execution that never quite reconciled the spiritual mysticism, or

mystical spiritualism, of the East, with the essentially Western practicality of the automobile. But their sheer numbers—278 dream cars in three years, still a world record today—previewed the vigor that marked Japan in the mid-Fifties as a rising giant on the automotive scene.

Slow to link the automobile with everyday applications, Japan's manufacturers perhaps dallied too long in an esoteric cloudland all their own. The **Jujitsu Swimboy Poolster** of 1955, for example, was inspired by a fourteenth-century etching of a lovely maiden staring at pond water. Swimming with driving, or for that matter driving while swimming, was nobody's known dream. Yet the Swimboy remains the only car of any kind to have totally solved the problem of top-down driving in the rain.

It was a business and cultural revolution: Twelve fiercely rivalrous auto makers joining to create one transcendent Japanese dream car, the only automobile ever inspired by the ancient creed of *juma-ha:* "Working as one, we split the costs and double the profit." No huzzahs greeted the debut of the **Hirsute Luckydog** on its 1956 debut, suggesting that perhaps twelve minds are not always better than

one. Its mixed if not colliding styling themes, three engines, and single seat attested in its absence to the vital importance of teamwork. But the fiasco was not in vain. Japanese car designers from the Hirsute forward have made a practice, if not a fetish, of checking in with one another on an almost minute-by-minute basis.

SWEDEN

Regard the vegetable garden on the hood of the one-of-a-kind **Vilmo,** Sweden's daring 1959 bid for dream-car immortality. Is this a health car, or is this a health car? The Vilmo branch of the Swedish Lung Club saw in the dream-car trend a publicity bonanza for exercise, clean living, and safety. Styling, comfort, speed—everything a driver could want was sacrificed to the greater good. The Vilmo's nonpolluting twin bicycle-type power systems led a panoply of health-related advances. Note the mighty twin filter tanks that actually *laundered* incoming air. Safety? Compressed-air flotation cylinders gave occupants a fighting chance for survival should the Vilmo find itself in one of those Scandinavian ferryboat sinkings. The Lung Club had hatched a smash hit Swedish-style. But perhaps the Vilmo got a trifle too much publicity. Spectators at the 1958 Malmo Social Uplift Show later spoke of a skulking figure amid the throng surrounding it that day, yet all stood agog as moments later the priceless sole prototype was ridden off its platform and out the door. It was never seen again.

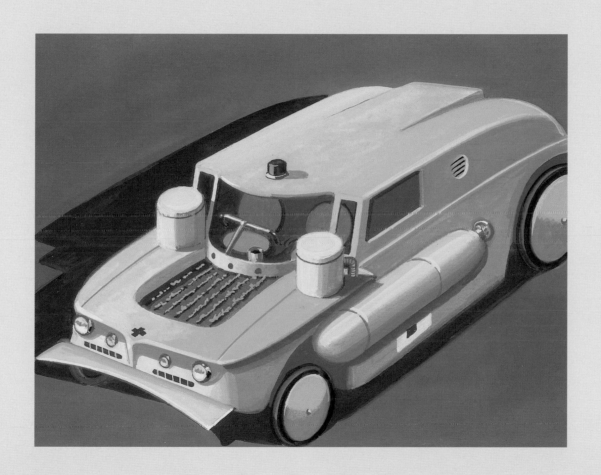

ABOUT THE AUTHOR

Beginning with his work for the *National Lampoon* in the early Seventies, Bruce McCall has published a prolific flow of parodic, satirical, and surreal humor, both written and illustrated, in almost every major publication in the United States and Canada. He has been a frequent contributor to *The New Yorker* since 1980 and regularly appears in *Vanity Fair*. His 1982 humor collection, *Zany Afternoons,* has become a collectors' item, and a 1999 show of his paintings at New York's James Goodman Gallery almost sold out. The Canadian-born McCall pursued careers in commercial art, automotive journalism, and advertising before yielding to a lifelong impulse and becoming a full-time humor freelancer in 1993. He considers himself first and foremost a writer, and published *Thin Ice,* his critically acclaimed memoir of growing up Canadian, in 1997. It has been made into a documentary by the National Film Board of Canada. Bruce McCall lives in New York City and is still a Canadian citizen.